WHAT CAN I SAY TO YOU, GOD?
VERSES FROM THE PSALMS ON PRAYER

BY ELSPETH CAMPBELL MURPHY
ILLUSTRATED BY JANE E. NELSON

Chariot Books

WHAT CAN I SAY TO YOU, GOD?
VERSES FROM THE PSALMS ON PRAYER

What can I say to you, God? What words can I use?

I can say I think you are wonderful. You are good, and what you do is good.

I will sing about how strong you are; I will sing about your love.

I can say thank you.
You cover the sky with clouds and send rain to make the grass grow green.

You give food to the animals and the wild, calling birds.

You send the icy winter and the soft, gentle spring. You made a beautiful world, and you tell us how to live in it.

But sometimes it's hard to tell you things, God . . . like when I've done things I know I shouldn't do. Then I say I'm sorry.

And you are kind and gentle. You don't get angry fast or stay angry long.

You forgive me. It's like you take the bad things I do and put them as far away as can be.

What else can I say to you, God?
I can say I trust you. You're like someone bigger who
holds my hand and shows me the way to go.

You're like a mother bird who cuddles her babies under her wings.

You're like a secret hideout that I can run to and be safe.

I can also say please help me. I'll pour out all that's bothering me. I'll tell you all my troubles.

I can say please help other people. Help them with their problems. Be near them when they're sad.

What can I say to you, God?
A lot!
And I know you will listen again, and again,
and again.

ii

Second Edition 1988
Third Edition 1989
Fourth Edition 1990
Fifth Edition 1990
Sixth Edition 1992
JS314704F

Instrument
Rating
Manual

Includes
Commercial Material

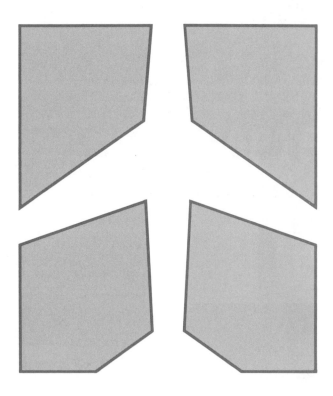

JEPPESEN
SANDERSON